Commissioned by the AMERICAN LISZT SOCIETY
in celebration of the 200th anniversary of the birth of FRANZ LISZT

First performance on February 18, 2011, by THOMAS HAMPSON and CRAIG RUTENBERG
at the Hugh Hodgson School of Music, the University of Georgia

Laura Sonnets

FRANCESCO PETRARCA
(1304–1374)

WILLIAM BOLCOM
(2010)

I. Sonetto 5

Andantino tranquillo; *stately* (♩ = c. 80)

Quan-do io mo-vo i so-

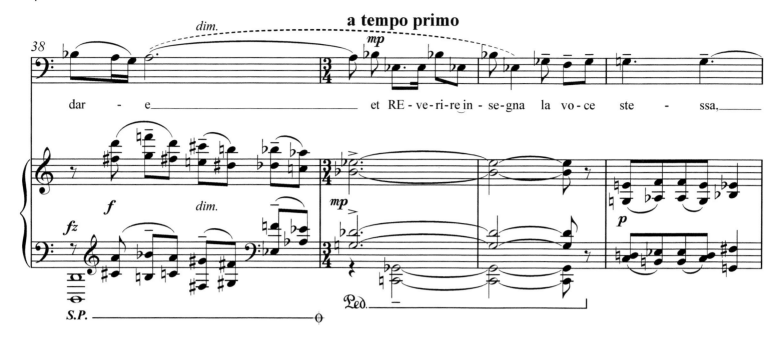

II. Sonetto 90

E-ra-no i ca-pei d'o-ro a l'au-ra spar-si_____ ch'en mil-le dol-ci no-di gli a-vol-ge_____ a,

e l' va-go lu-me ol-tra mi-su-ra ar-de_____ a_____ di quel be-gli oc-chi, ch'or ne son sì scar-si;

e'l vi-so di pie-to-si co-lor' far-si,_____ (non so se ve-ro o fal-so) mi pa-re_____ a:

i' che l'es-ca a-mo-ro-sa al pet-to a-ve_____ a,_____ qual me-ra-vig-lia se di su-bi-to

8

III. Sonetto 267

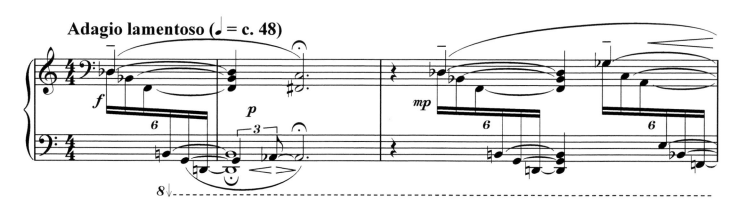

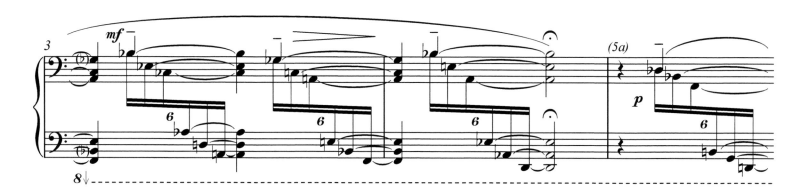

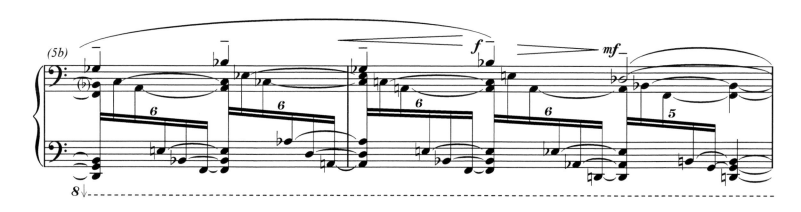

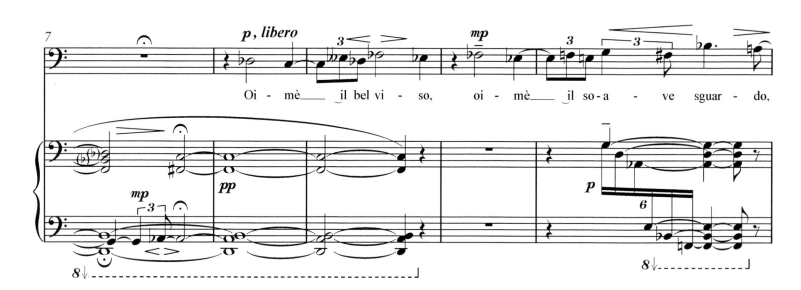

Oi - mè___ il bel vi - so, oi - mè___ il so-a - ve sguar - do,

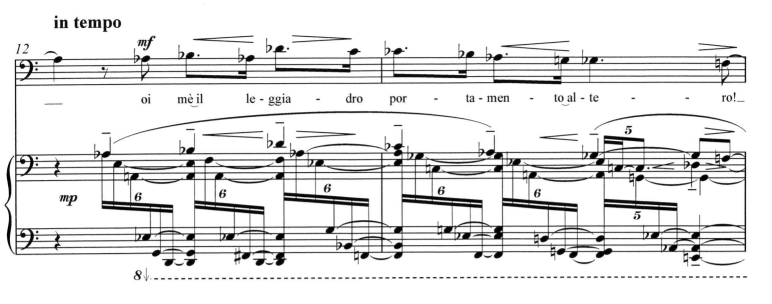

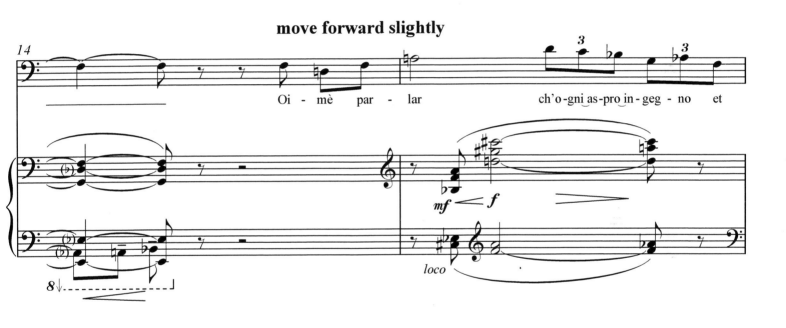

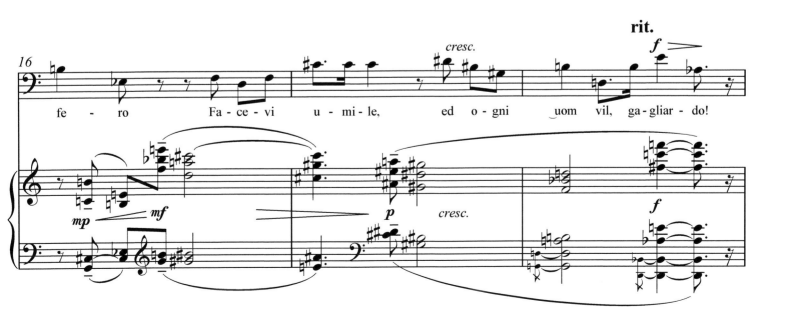

* In this case the "t" is sounded; the "t" in "et" before a consonant is silent. (It is now thought that in Petrarch's day the "t" in "et" was sounded like the "d" in "ed," as in modern Italian.)

IV. Sonetto 286

Gently (♩. = 94); *moving forward*

Se quel-l'au - ra so-a-ve de' so-
spi - ri_____ ch'i' o - do_____ di co-lei_____ chi fu_____ mi a
don - na_____ (or è in Cie - lo *et an - cor par qui

*See p. 10.

V. Sonetto 292

TEXTS AND TRANSLATIONS

I. SONETTO 5

Quando io movo i sospiri a chiamar voi
e 'l nome che nel cor mi scrisse Amore,
LAU-dando s'incomincia udir di fore
il suon de' primi dolci accenti suoi;   4

vostro stato RE-al che 'ncontro poi
raddoppia a l'alta impresa il mio valore;
ma "TA-ci," grida il fin, "ché farle onore
è d'altri omeri soma che da' tuoi."   8

Così LAU-dare et RE-verire insegna
la voce stessa, pur ch' altri vi chiami,
o d'ogni reverenza et d'onor degna;   11

se non che forse Apollo si disdegna
ch'a parlar de' suoi sempre verdi rami
lingua mor-TA-l presuntuosa vegna.   14

When I move my sighs to call you and the name that Love wrote on my heart, the sound of its first sweet accents is heard without in LAU-ds.

Your RE-gal state, which I meet next, redoubles my strength for the high enterprise; but "TA-lk no more!" cries the ending, "for to do her honor is a burden for other shoulders than yours."

Thus the word itself teaches LAU-d and RE-verence, whenever anyone calls you, O Lady worthy of all reverence and honor;

except that perhaps Apollo is incensed that any mor-TA-l tongue should come presumptuous to speak of his eternally green boughs.

The poem plays on the syllables of Laura's name, in a Latinized version, Laureta, of the French Laurette.
eternally green boughs: the evergreen laurel, with an allusion to the myth of Apollo and Daphne. Daphne, the daughter of the god of the river Peneus in Thessaly, was pursued by Apollo. She prayed to her father to preserve her virginity, and when Apollo caught up with her she was transformed into a laurel. Apollo adopted the tree as his own and crowned himself with a wreath from it. (Ovid, *Metamorphoses* 1.452-567.) The laurel was supposedly immune from lightning. Its Latin name, *laurus*, was thought to derive from the verb *laudare* (to praise). Petrarch considered it the crown both of poets and of triumphing emperors.

II. SONETTO 90

Erano i capei d'oro a l'aura sparsi
che 'n mille dolci nodi gli avolgea,
e 'l vago lume oltra misura ardea
di quei begli occhi, ch' or ne son sì scarsi;   4

e 'l viso di pietosi color farsi
(non so se vero o falso) mi parea:
i' che l'esca amorosa al petto avea,
qual meraviglia se di subito arsi?   8

Non era l'andar suo cosa mortale
ma d'angelica forma, et le parole
sonavan altro che pur voce umana: 11

uno spirto celeste, un vivo sole
fu quel ch' i' vidi, et se non fosse or tale,
piaga per allentar d'arco non sana.   14

Her golden hair was loosed to the breeze, which turned it in a thousand sweet knots, and the lovely light burned without measure in her eyes, which are now so stingy of it;

and it seemed to me (I know not whether truly or falsely) her face took on the color of pity: I, who had the tinder of love in my breast, what wonder is it if I suddenly caught fire?

Her walk was not that of a mortal thing but of some angelic form, and her words sounded different from a merely human voice:

a celestial spirit, a living sun was what I saw, and if she were not such now, a wound is not healed by the loosening of the bow.

III. SONETTO 267

Oimè il bel viso, oimè il soave sguardo,
oimè il leggiadro portamento altero!
Oimè il parlar ch' ogni aspro ingegno et fero
facevi umile ed ogni uom vil, gagliardo!   4

Et oimè il dolce riso onde uscio 'l dardo
di che morte, altro bene omai non spero!
Alma real dignissima d'impero
se non fossi fra noi scesa sì tardo: 8

per voi conven ch' io arda e 'n voi respiro,
ch' i' pur fui vostro; et se di voi son privo
via men d'ogni sventura altra mi dole;   11

di speranza m'empieste et di desire
quand' io parti' dal sommo piacer vivo,
ma 'l vento ne portava le parole.   14

Alas the lovely face, alas the gentle glance, alas the proud, carefree bearing! Alas the speech that made every harsh or savage mind humble and every base man valiant!

And alas the sweet smile whence came forth the dart from which now I expect death, no other good! Regal soul, worthy of empire if you had not come down among us so late:

for you I must burn, in you breathe, for I have been only yours; and if I am deprived of you, it pains me more than any other misfortune;

with hope you filled me and with desire, when I left still alive that highest pleasure, but the wind carried off the words.

IV. SONETTO 286

Se quell'aura soave de' sospiri
ch' i' odo di colei che qui fu mia
donna (or è in Cielo et ancor par qui sia
et viva et senta et vada et ami et spiri)   4

ritrar potessi, or che caldi desiri
movrei parlando, sì gelosa et pia
torna ov' io son, temendo non fra via
mi stanchi o 'ndietro o da man manca giri.   8

Ir dritto alto m'insegna, et io, che 'ntendo
le sue caste lusinghe e i giusti preghi
col dolce mormorar pietoso et basso,   11

secondo lei conven mi regga et pieghi,
per la dolcezza che del suo dir prendo,
ch' avria vertù di far piangere un sasso.   14

If I could portray the gentle breath of the sighs that I hear from her who here was my lady (now she is in Heaven but seems to be here and to live and feel and walk and love and breathe),

oh what hot desires would I move by speaking! so assiduous and kind she returns where I am, fearing lest I become weary along the way or turn back or to the left.

She teaches me to go straight up, and I, who understand her chaste allurements and her just prayers with their sweet, low, pitying murmur,

I must rule and bend myself according to her because of the sweetness I take from her words, which would have the power to make a stone weep.

V. SONETTO 292

Gli occhi di ch' io parlai sì caldamente,
et le braccia et le mani e i piedi e 'l viso
che m'avean sì da me stesso diviso
et fatto singular da l'altra gente,   4

le crespe chiome d'or puro lucente
e 'l lampeggiar de l'angelico riso
che solean fare in terra un paradiso,
poca polvere son che nulla sente.   8

Et io pur vivo, onde mi doglio et sdegno,
rimaso senza 'l lume ch' amai tanto
in gran fortuna e 'n disarmato legno.   11

Or sia qui fine al mio amoroso canto;
secca è la vena de l'usato ingegno,
et la cetera mia rivolta in pianto.   14

Those eyes of which I spoke so warmly, and the arms and the hands and the feet and the face that had so estranged me from myself and isolated me from other people,

the curling locks of pure shining gold, and the lightning of the angelic smile that used to make a paradise on earth, all are a bit of dust that feels nothing.

And I still live, at which I am sorrowful and angry, left without the light I loved so, in a great tempest and a dismasted ship.

Now here let there be an end to my song of love; dry is the vein of my accustomed wit, and my lyre is turned to weeping.

NOTE FOR LAURA SONNETS

No one seems to know whether the Laura in the sonnets of Francesco Petrarca (1304-1374), known as Petrarch, was a real person, something we do seem to know about his friend Dante's muse, Beatrice. Idealized women as a concept date at least from Eleanor d'Aquitaine; this allows and leads to the possibility of mere poetic conceit in Petrarch's sonnets, in that Laura's name becomes a source of word games and (sober) puns, and the violent emotions the *Rime sparse* seem at first to be so full of are actually less central to the poems' meaning than if we look to the sheer artifice of their elegant construction. But this would be to deny the profound feeling and wealth of nuance in these sonnets.

I think that the miracle of these foundational works is of perfect balance between emotion and artifice. In this context it doesn't matter whether Laura ever actually existed. But if she did or did not exist in the flesh, she exists now in these sonnets as indubitably as does Bernini's Daphne at Rome's Villa Borghese, caught in stone as she turns into a laurel tree. I feel these settings should be performed with great restraint and nuance, so that the balance between art and emotion becomes the fulcrum and focus of the songs.

William Bolcom